4 Multicultural Bedtime Stories

4 Multicultural Bedtime Stories for Wide-Awake Kids
by Karl Beckstrand
ISBN: 978-1951599294

FIND the birds, camel, crickets, dragon, fish, lamb, moth, mouse, mosquito, 2 cats, 2 dogs, 1 red panda & many constellations.

The Bridge of the Golden Wood: A Parable on How to Earn a Living (Careers for Kids series)
Copyright © 2004 Karl Beckstrand, illustrations by Karl Beckstrand & Yaniv Cahoua
LCCN: 2016949820, ISBN: 978-1536889864

Sounds in the House - Sonidos en la casa: A Mystery (find this book cover inside a below story!)
Copyright © 2004 Karl Beckstrand, illustration copyright © 2004 Channing Jones
ISBN: 978-0615442303
Available in English-only, Spanish, bilingual (with pronunciation guide) soft, hard, and ebook versions

Bright Star, Night Star: An Astronomy Story (Careers for Kids series)
Text copyright © 2014 Karl Beckstrand, illustration copyright © 2014 Luis F. Sanz
LCCN: 2013913403, ISBN: 978-0985398880

Why Juan Can't Sleep: A Funny Mystery
Text Copyright © 2010 Karl Beckstrand, illustration copyright © 2012 Luis F. Sanz
LCCN: 2012914948, ISBN: 978-0615692296

Premio Publishing & Gozo Books   Midvale, UT, USA
© 2024. All rights reserved. This book, or parts thereof, may not be reproduced or shared in any form—except by reviewer, who may quote brief passages or sample illustrations in a printed, online, or broadcast review—without prior written permission from the publisher. Derechos reservados. Queda prohibida la reproducción o transmisión de parte alguna de esta obra, sin permiso escrito del publicador.

ORDER direct, or via major book distributors

FREE ebooks, lesson plans, exclusive book bundles, and online SECRETS:

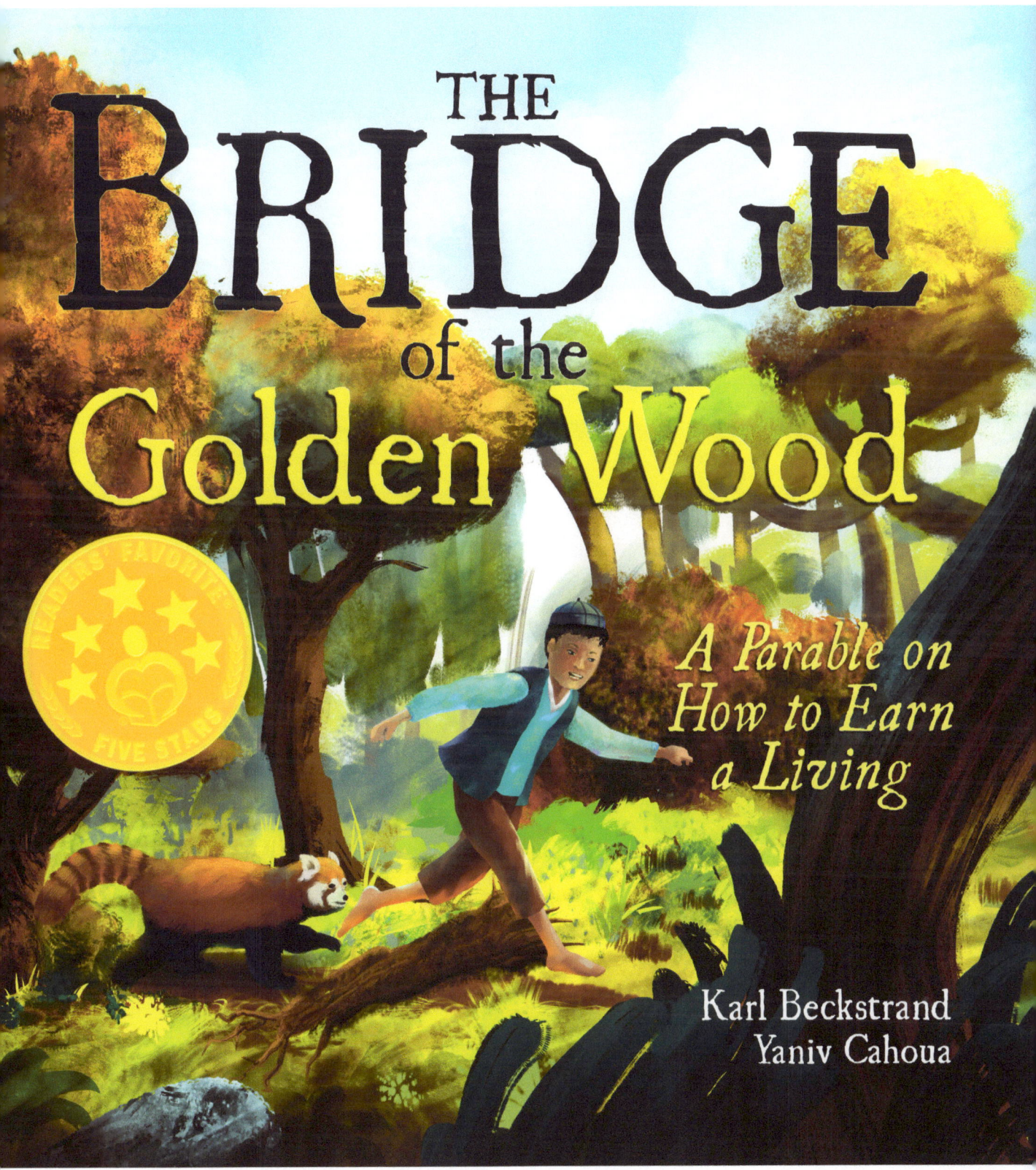

THE BRIDGE of the Golden Wood

A Parable on How to Earn a Living

Karl Beckstrand
Yaniv Cahoua

The Bridge of the Golden Wood

Premio Publishing & Gozo Books
Midvale, UT, USA
Library of Congress Control Number: 2016949820
ISBN: 978-1536889864
ASIN: B01N0XCPQK
Illustrations by Yaniv Cahoua & Karl Beckstrand
Book 4 in **Careers for Kids** series; Copyright © 2017 Karl Beckstrand

For Dad, who never feared work but also took time to play

All rights reserved: This book, or parts thereof, may not be reproduced or shared in any form—except by reviewer, who may quote brief passages or sample illustrations in a printed, online, or broadcast review—without prior written permission from the publisher. Derechos reservados. Queda prohibida la reproducción o transmisión de parte alguna de esta obra, sin permiso escrito del publicador. Nothing herein is intended as legal or investment advice.

Other books/ebooks by Karl Beckstrand:
Agnes's Rescue, Ida's Witness, Anna's Prayer, Samuel Sailing (nonfiction)
She Doesn't Want the Worms! – ¡Ella no quiere los gusanos!
Crumbs on the Stairs – Migas en las escaleras: A Mystery
No Offense: Communication Guaranteed Not to Offend
Sounds in the House – Sonidos en la casa: A Mystery
The Dancing Flamingos of Lake Chimichanga
GROW! How We Get Food from Our Garden
Horse & Dog Adventures in Early California
Bright Star, Night Star: An Astronomy Story
Polar Bear Bowler: A Story Without Words
Arriba Up, Abajo Down at the Boardwalk
Bad Bananas: A Story Cookbook for Kids
Butterfly Blink: A Book Without Words
Gopher Golf: A Wordless Picture Book
Why Juan Can't Sleep: A Mystery?
Ma MacDonald Flees the Farm

ORDER direct, or via major distributors. Libros online books FREE/GRATIS

KidsWorldBooks.com

He always carried tools with him—and he usually had a rope nearby (it was handy for swinging, hauling, and securing things).

One day as the boy was playing along a stream near his home, he noticed an old woman he had never seen before. She was sitting on the bank—looking intently at a mass of branches that the water had piled against some rocks in the stream.

"Hello," said the boy, curious to know who she was—and why she stared so intently at the dead wood.
"Hello," said the old woman, not taking her eyes from the branches.
"What are you looking at?" asked the boy.
"Trouble and treasure," she said.

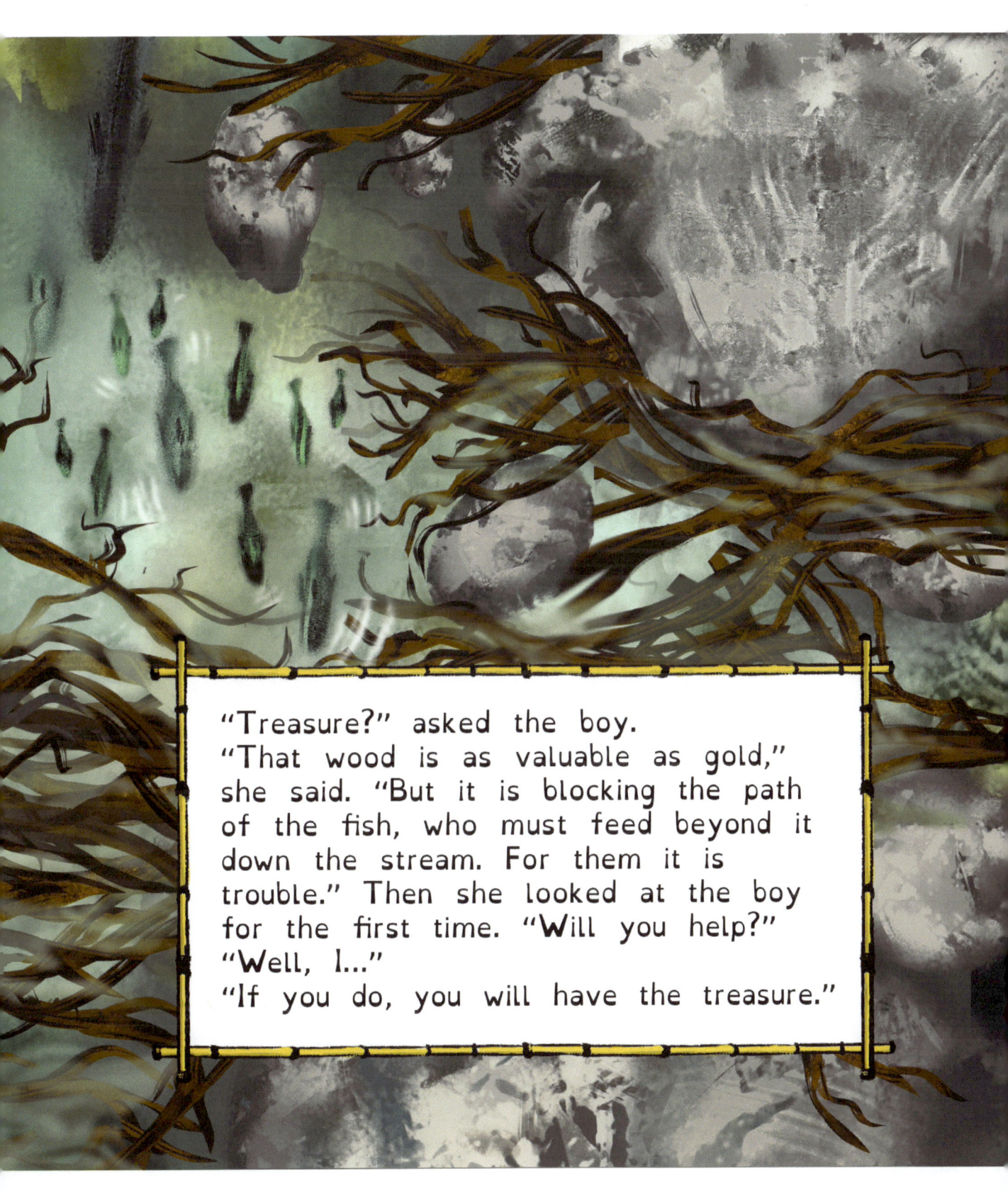

"Treasure?" asked the boy.
"That wood is as valuable as gold," she said. "But it is blocking the path of the fish, who must feed beyond it down the stream. For them it is trouble." Then she looked at the boy for the first time. "Will you help?"
"Well, I..."
"If you do, you will have the treasure."

The clever boy needed no more encouragement. He already had a plan. He quickly climbed a tree to retrieve his swinging rope.

The old woman smiled as the boy sat on the bank and took off his shoes. "Excuse, me," he said, turning back to the woman. "How will I know when I've found the treas..."

There was no one there—only a splash in the water and the tailfin of a fish going under it.

The boy looked around and peered into the nearby bushes. "Well," he said, rolling up his sleeves, "at least I can help the fish get to their food." The boy waded into the stream and began to gather the branches and lift them on top of the rocks they were pinned against. He was able to wrap his rope under and over them until they were in a large, tidy bundle supported by the rocks that had once trapped them.

As he tied some knots, he noticed eager fish swimming around and past him under his bundle of branches.

Just as the boy was leaving the water, a man with a large sack on his back approached the stream. "I'll give you a gold coin," he said, "if you let me across your bridge."

"My bridge?" said the boy. "Ah, of course! Please come across." The man thanked him and gave him a small coin of gold before going on his way.

Every day after that many travelers and peddlers came across the boy's bridge, and each of them gave the boy gold (which his parents let him keep, since his idea and effort had created the source of the income).

The boy spent many a happy day playing along the stream, watching the fish feed, and earning money to feed his family. He never saw the old woman again.

What did the boy do that helped him to find the treasure? How might you find treasure in trouble?
Problems and needs are opportunities to help and can lead to income. See opportunity in every obstacle. Can you solve problems or serve people? Then you can earn money—even pay for your living expenses and those of others. What if you see a need, fill it, but don't get paid? Are you sure you weren't paid? How do you feel helping someone? Pretty good, huh? (Some people pay with things or via service.) Even without pay, you gain a reputation as a worker, a problem solver—plus you get experience to make you more valuable to future customers (you may also get ideas for products/services that could earn money in the future). Some ideas below may not be suitable for where you live or for someone your age; be sure to have an adult go over your plans before you begin a project (also see local and country business laws). The only guarantee of success is what you guarantee yourself through your imagination, effort, and persistence.

EARNING IDEAS	EXAMPLES
Make something to sell.	Cupcakes, an app, a shoe rack, soap, kites
Clean, fix, or repurpose something.	Bicycles, windows, furniture, appliances, tools
Collect something to sell.	Stamps, coins, books, games, antiques, wood, fruit
Create something to sell.	Photographs, paintings, music, fonts, games, crafts
Grow/raise something to sell.	Watermelon, lavender, nuts, sheep, pets
Recycle for cash.	Metal, glass, plastic, electronics, paper, clothes
Rent things to people who need them.	Property, tools, vehicles, ad space, electronics
Trade things for something more valuable to you.	Toys for games, electronics, clothes, or collectibles
Sell/give something extra you can spare.	Books, toys, games, clothes, gadgets
Sell other people's product to earn a percentage.	Candles, cookies, apps, magazines, ad space
Perform/entertain.	Sing/dance/act/play a musical instrument, do magic
Publish a book/ebook, then...	Teach classes, speak to groups, write a blog or a newsletter, share information via video/audio/Web
Research & share information.	
Participate/share your opinion for a reward.	Surveys, polls, focus groups, studies, mystery shop
Transport things for compensation.	Pets, people, recyclables, junk, wood, garbage cans

WORK FOR SOMEONE ELSE

Work for a friend, family member, or company—or provide a specific service to many people/clients as a contractor (some work requires a license and/or permits).

As you get older and wiser, your opportunities to earn money increase. There is ALWAYS work to be found or something that needs fixing/improving. Perhaps the only job you see is not the kind of work you prefer; consider taking it for the experience and to network (meet new people and learn of other opportunities).

EXAMPLES

Paper route, walk/groom pets, run errands, child care, wash & detail cars, clean houses, move furniture, chop wood, repair bikes. Some things—like mowing lawns/landscaping, raking leaves, or shoveling snow—are seasonal and can replace other seasonal activities.

TIP: If a company you want to work for isn't hiring, consider volunteering your time. This way, you will gain experience and the company will see what a good worker you can be.

START A BUSINESS OR FRANCHISE

Solve a problem/provide goods or services that meet people's needs. Seek expert input. Get a business license and tax ID.

- For best results, continue to study business, computers, spelling, grammar, math, speaking, marketing, business law—and the industries that interest you.
- Never sell something that isn't yours unless you have permission from the owners to do so (even art and ideas).
- As your business grows, hire a team of hardworking people (especially those with skills you don't possess).
- Always plan your work; write specific goals and steps! Be flexible and creative. Make house calls. Work. Do your best. Be helpful—even if there seems to be no reward. Find partners with integrity. Budget your time and money. Keep your word. Be positive. Make decisions based on the best facts available (know your industry!). Constantly improve. Take care of your health. Be honest. Be Kind.

EXAMPLES

Build web sites, sell products or services online, review/rate organizations, clean homes/offices, build things/buildings, promote other people's products/services, connect like-minded people (create an association/newsletter/conference), invent a life-simplifying product, create an app that tracks spending or caloric intake or gives other information, repair electronics/appliances/vehicles/furniture, transport people/things, teach other people to do something that you have done.

TIP: Be sure you can trust the people you work for and with. Signed agreements can help you avoid some conflicts.

TIP: Education can make a great difference in your earnings; it doesn't have to be a college degree; consider trade schools, self study, and apprenticeships. Some companies will train you. (Travel is a great education too!) Each person has gifts that need to be discovered to help others and self. With practice, something you thought you were bad at may become your greatest ability.

SEE: ChildrenEarn.com for information on finding customers, managing money, and moving up in an organization. **Like this book?** *Please comment online!* **More Careers for Kids books:** *Great Cape o' Colors - Capa de colores; Bright Star, Night Star: An Astronomy Story; Ma MacDonald Flees the Farm: It's Not a Pretty Picture...Book*

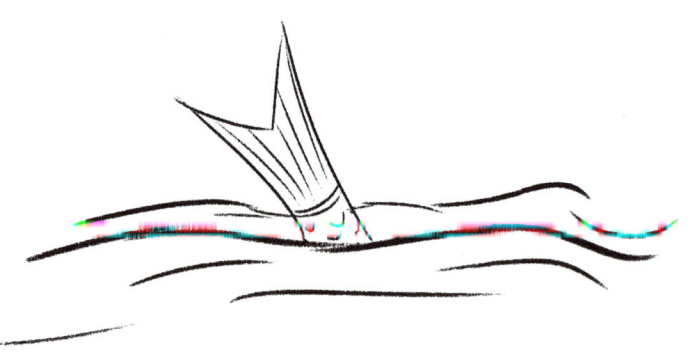

Sounds in the House
Sonidos en la casa

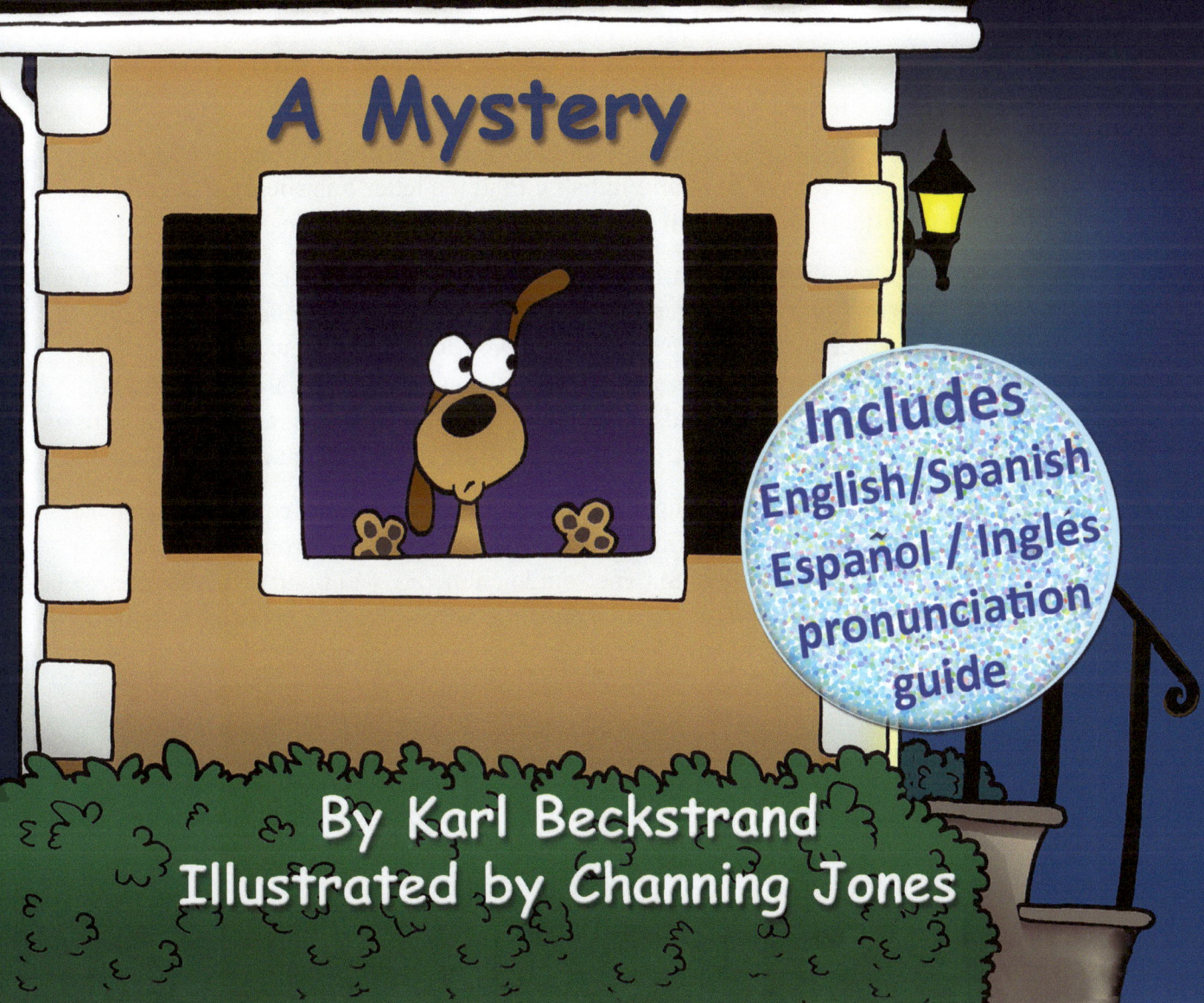

A Mystery

Includes English/Spanish Español / Inglés pronunciation guide

By Karl Beckstrand
Illustrated by Channing Jones

Sounds in the House
Sonidos en la casa
A Mystery

BANG!
CLACK!
CREEK!

This book is available in English, Spanish, and ebook versions: KidsWorldBooks.com

Spanish vowels have one sound each: a = *ah* e = *eh* i = *ee* o = *oh* u = *oo*. Every vowel should be pronounced (except for the **u** after a **q** [*que* is pronounced *keh*]). In Spanish, the letter **j** is pronounced as an English **h** (and the letter **h** is silent), **ll** sounds like a **y** (or a **j** in some countries), and **ñ** has an **ny** sound (*año* sounds like *ah-nyo*).

Spanish nouns are masculine or feminine and are usually preceded by an article: *la* = feminine *the*; *el* = masculine *the; una* = feminine *a* or *one; un* = masculine *a* or *one*. Articles (and –*s/-es* after nouns) reflect plural: *las* = plural feminine *the; los* = plural masculine *the; unas* = feminine *some; unos* = masculine *some*. In Spanish, the accent is generally on the first or second syllable of simple words. Words with four or more syllables often have the accent on the third syllable. Variations occur with conjugation. If there's an accent mark—follow that!

Las combinaciones de letras en ingles pueden cambiar los sonidos por completo: **ck** se pronuncia como **k;** **wr** se pronuncia como **r**; **ee** se pronuncia **i**; **qu** se pronuncia **cu**; **ai** se pronuncia **ey**; **ll** se pronuncia **l**; y **gh** no tiene sonido en medio, y al final, de la mayoría de las palabras. El sonido de **ch** (de *chico*) se ocupa en el medio y al final de las palabras también. Para pronunciar **sh**, mantén la mandíbula cerrada y los labios abiertos; sopla aire entre los dientes (al añadir la vocal que le siga, si hay.) Para pronunciar **th**, pon la lengua entre los dientes de adelante (arriba y abajo) y sopla un poquito de aire sobre la lengua.

Los sustantivos en inglés no tienen género; se usa *the* para *la*, *el*, *las*, y *los*. Algunas palabras en ingles — a pesar de escribirse de forma diferente — terminan con el mismo sonido (se pronuncian como si se escribieran igual al final): *guy* y *pie*, *do* y *boo*, *throw* y *go*, *trees* y *breeze*.

Premio Publishing & Gozo Books
Text Copyright © 2016 Karl Beckstrand
Illustration Copyright © 2016 Channing Jones
Find the dog, moth, cat, flowers, mouse & boy.

Midvale, UT, USA
ISBN: 978-0615442303
ORDER via major distributors
Online books FREE/gratis: KidsWorldBooks.com

I hear a noise,
SOUNDS in the house!

Escucho un ruido,
¡SONIDOS en la casa!

A squeak from the door,
steps on the floor,
a creak on the stair,

IT'S RAISING MY HAIR!

Un chirrido desde la puerta, pasos en el piso, un rechinar desde el escalón. ¡Los pelos se me levantan del temor!

El reloj hace tic tac.
Una polilla golpea contra la ventana.

The clock ticks.
A moth taps my window.

The water
heater goes,
TAT TAT TAT

El calentador
de agua dice:
TATO TATO

OH, THAT CAT!
¡Oh, ese gato!

Las cañerías gimen. El refrigerador zzzzumba.

Pipes moan. The refrigerator HUMMMMMS.

Trees creak in the breeze.

Los árboles rechinan en la brisa.

BUMP! BOOP! BLOP! BING!

Algo corre sobre el techo!

Something scurries across the roof.

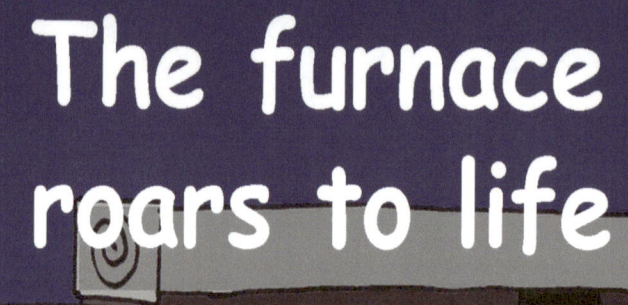

The furnace roars to life

El calefactor brama con vida

Y hace gruñir al perro.

...and makes a dog Growl!

Is someone in the garage?

¿Hay alguien en el garaje?

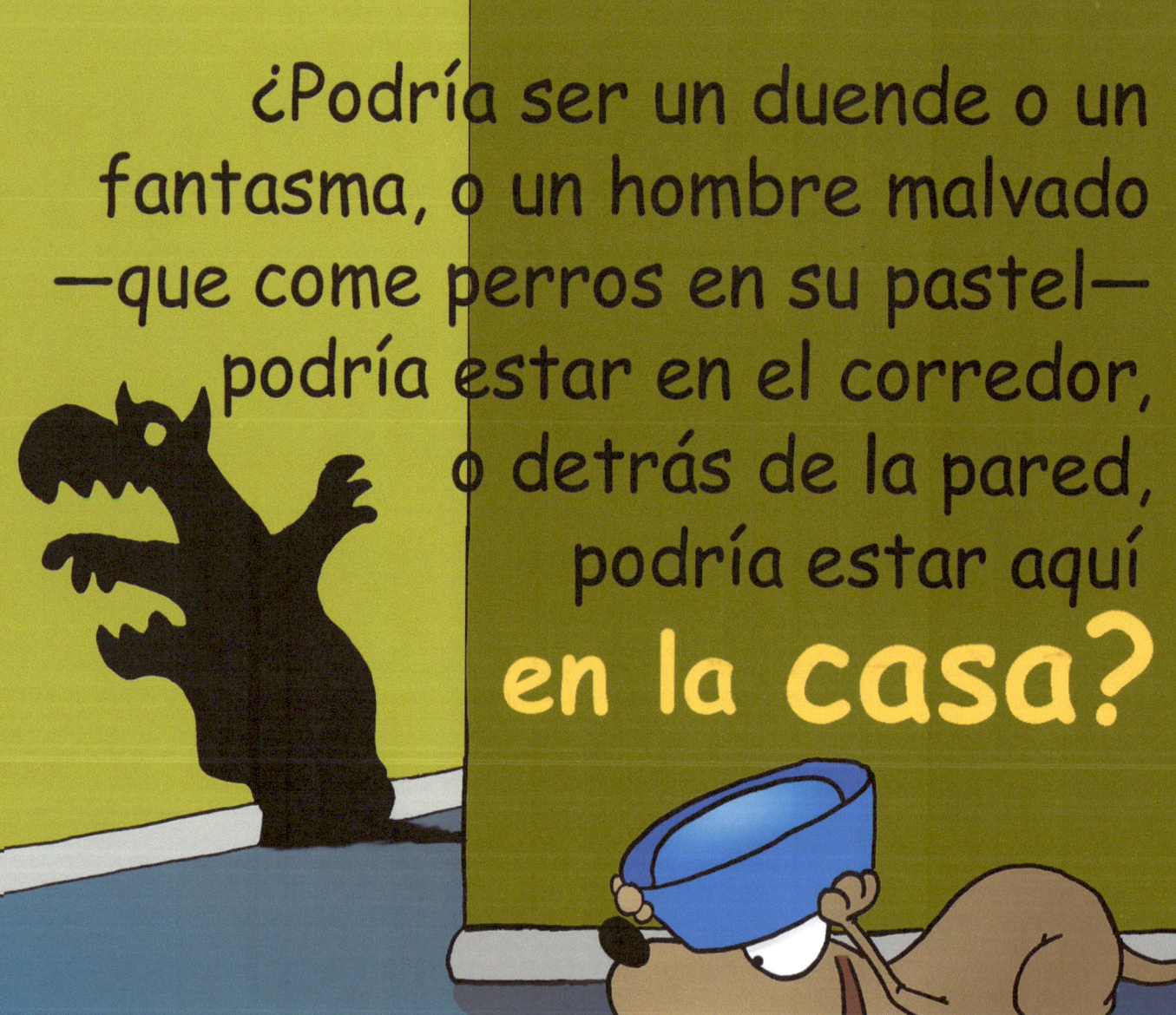

¿Podría ser un duende o un fantasma, o un hombre malvado —que come perros en su pastel— podría estar en el corredor, o detrás de la pared, podría estar aquí **en la casa?**

Could it be that a goblin or
ghost, or a really bad guy
—who eats dogs in his pie—
may be down the hall,
or behind the wall,
could be
here in our house?

O quizás sea un ratón.

Or, perhaps it's a mouse.

I think I know just what to do! I'll throw down the covers, and yell...

Yo creo saber exactamente qué hacer. Me quitaré las frazadas y gritaré:

WHY JUAN CAN'T SLEEP

A Funny Mystery

Karl Beckstrand   Luis F. Sanz

Why Juan Can't Sleep: A Mystery?

Premio Publishing & Gozo Books
Midvale, UT, USA
Library of Congress Catalog No.: 2012914948

Text Copyright © 2012 Karl Beckstrand
Illustration Copyright © 2012 Luis F. Sanz

All rights reserved: This book, or parts thereof, may not be reproduced or shared in any form—except by reviewer, who may quote brief passages or sample illustrations in a printed, online, or broadcast review—without prior written permission from the publisher. Derechos reservados. Queda prohibida la reproducción o transmisión de esta obra, sin permiso escrito del publicador.

FIND the bear, lamb, camel, dragon, dog, crickets, mosquito, cat, bird, and rabbit.

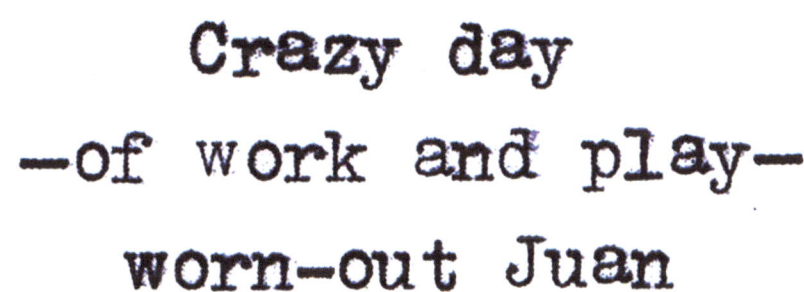

Crazy day
—of work and play—
worn-out Juan

Tonight he won't be counting lambies. poop-ed-ness fills the air.

It brings him full alert!

There's a draft from the shaft and drips in the sink.

WWAAAAAA

drip drip drip

Now my sister wants a drink.

Punching his pillow,
Juan settles again.

...AND THE NUMBER ONE THING THAT KEEPS PEOPLE UP AT NIGHT IS...

Itches...twitches;
he picks at his stitches.
He thinks about riches.

he's dreaming of
WITCHES!

BUT FRITO... I'D RATHER HE FED!

A plane, a train,
thunder and rain,
police in the lane...

URP! LAST NIGHT'S LO MEIN.

He counts in his brain,

THE STRAIN, THE PAIN!

(he's bursting a vein)
—He's going insane.

There's a ghost
in the glow!

NO, A DANCE OF THE PANTS

"I'll give this bed just one more chance!"

Darned drumming and dancing, driving and drooling, dripping, drinking, dragging, drilling, doggie droning...

TELEPHONING!

BRI...NG!!!!

¡BASTA!

(which means, ENOUGH!)

dragging,
droopy,
...dreamland?

Find these constellations inside

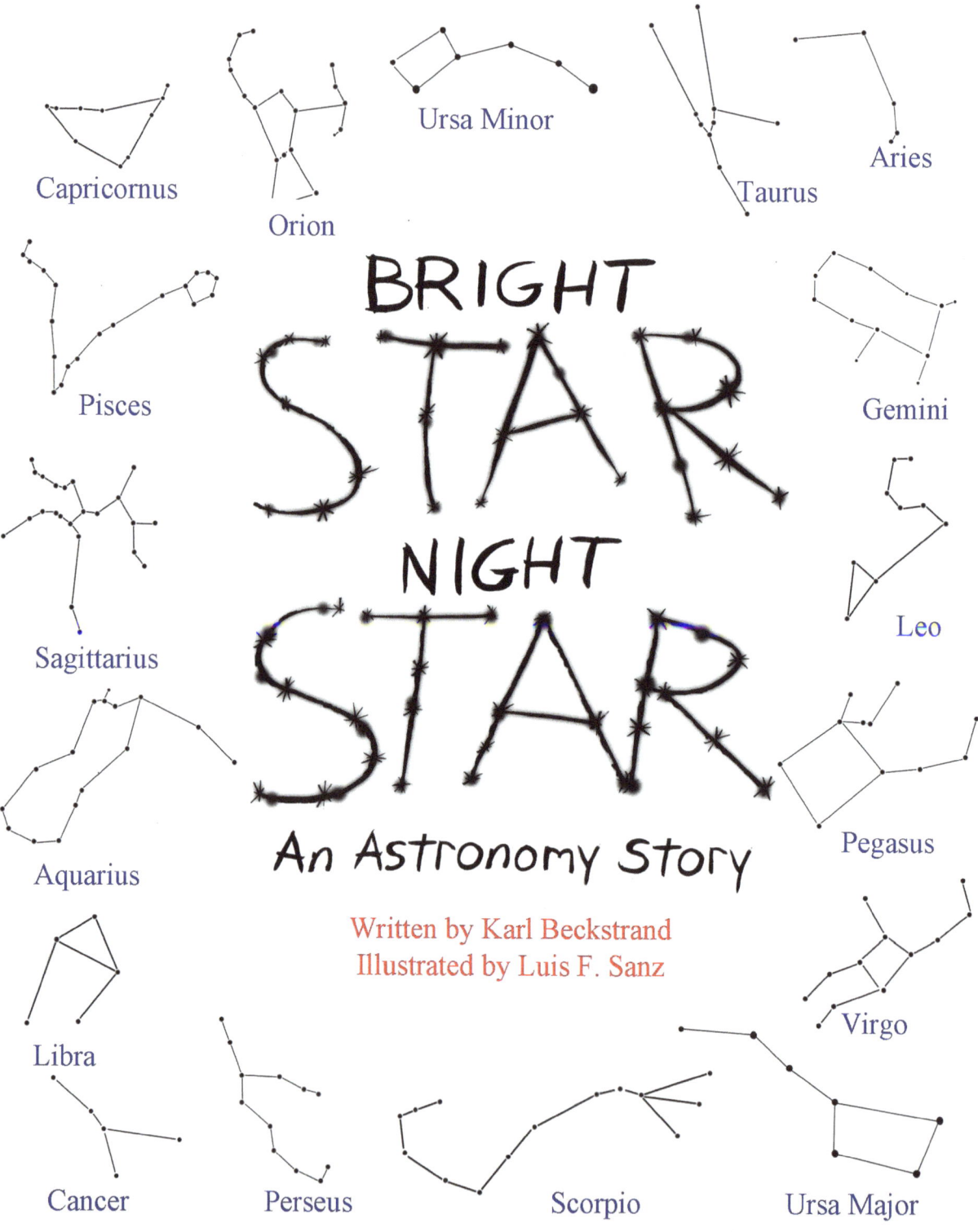

BRIGHT STAR NIGHT STAR

An Astronomy Story

Written by Karl Beckstrand
Illustrated by Luis F. Sanz

Winking stars, blinking stars—
twinkling stars too—
stars have crowns we call "coronas."
Kings have crowns, do you?

Blazar, quasar, variable stars,
red stars, white stars,
Earth, moon, Mars . . .

Mercury, Neptune, Jupiter, Venus, Saturn, Pluto, Europa, Uranus.

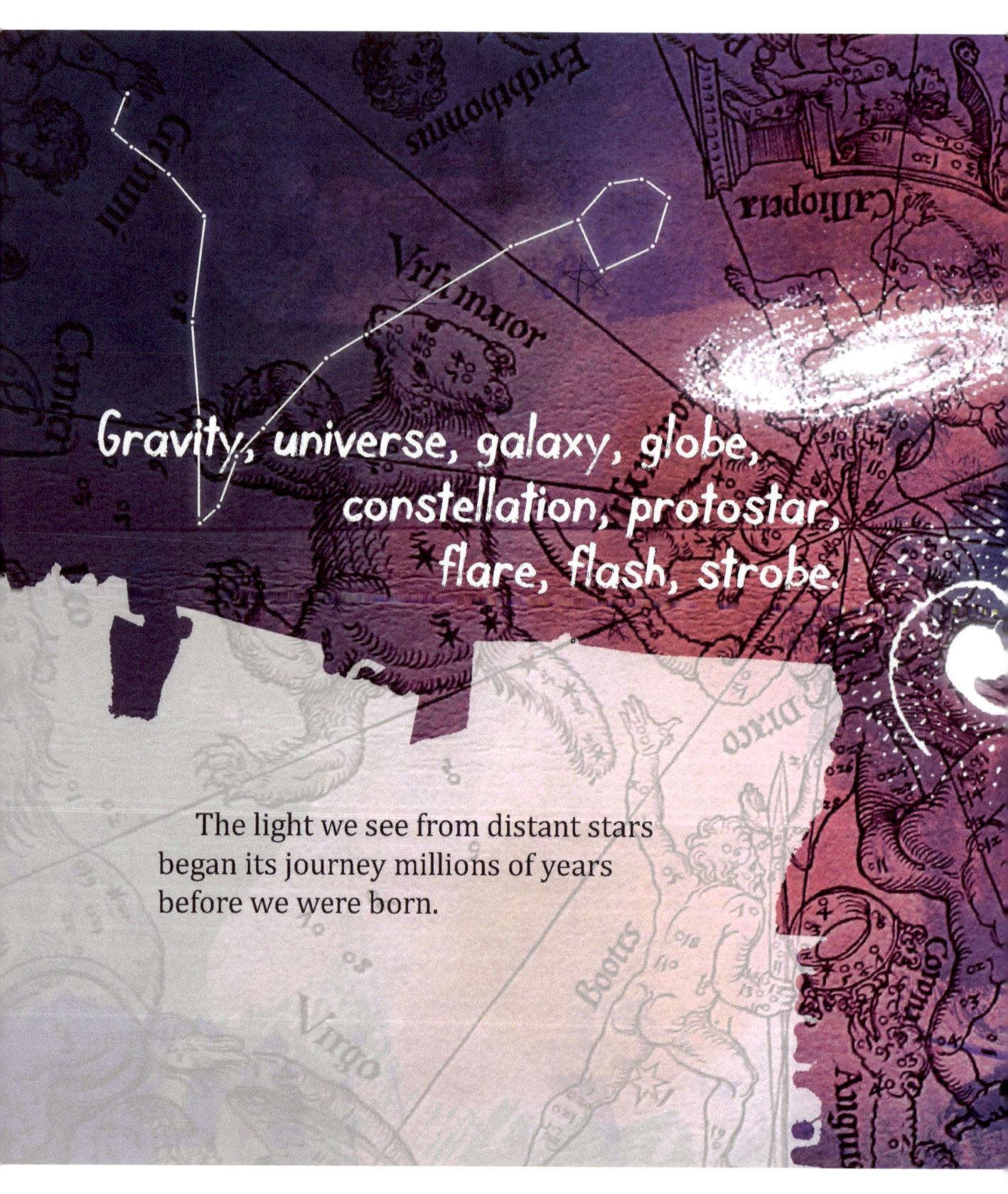

Gravity, universe, galaxy, globe, constellation, protostar, flare, flash, strobe.

The light we see from distant stars began its journey millions of years before we were born.

Our sun is a yellow star,
dark brings out its light.
Have you wished upon a star—
first one that you sight?

Star chart, star clock,
supernova, light year,
seasons, solstice, telescope, calendar.

Stars can help us find our way.
They can help us count the Mays.
Months, minutes, hours, days—
we can't make them stay.

To find the North Star, make a line between the last two stars of the Big Dipper (cup end--see cover). Follow that line up, out of the cup, to a bright star (the end of the Little Dipper handle). That star, "Polaris," shows which way is north.

Red dwarf, white dwarf,
black hole, brown dwarf,
gas giant, blue giant,
blue straggler, red giant.

Eclipse, equinox,
solar wind, and storm,
sunset, sparkling,
luminous, warm.

Glimmering, shimmering,
sunlit, soaring things—
objects on dark velvet—
fly on unseen wings.

Stars that beam, stars in stream,
seem to glow and gleam,
brilliant orbs, floating rings
in our deepest dreams.

Matter, meteor, starburst, void,
planet, comet, asteroid,
nova, nebula, neutron, night,
Milky Way, northern lights.

Fire, furnace, stars that grow—
never asking why—
cluster, luster, stars like snow,
diamonds in the sky.

(The skies are full of more stars than you or I could count in a hundred million years—dawning, dying, and blooming anew.

Some stars live ten billion years. But you are older than the stars. You and I are made of stardust. We will go on forever.)

www.ingramcontent.com/pod-product-compliance
Lightning Source LLC
Chambersburg PA
CBHW041511220426
43661CB00047B/1535